A Child's First Library of Learning

Animals in Action

TIME-LIFE BOOKS • ALEXANDRIA, VIRGINIA

Contents

? Do Moths and Butterflies Have Eyes on Their Wings?

ANSWER 1 Some moths have markings on their rear wings that look like large eyes. Usually the moth hides them, but when it's attacked the moth shows them to frighten the attacker.

Here it is.

The bird was going to eat the moth until it saw the markings shaped like large eyes. When those suddenly appeared, the bird was frightened and flew away.

■ The hawkmoth

The eye-shaped markings of the hawkmoth usually can't be seen because they're hidden by the moth's front wings. And since the front wings are the same color as the leaves of a tree, the moth can blend in with its surroundings. When the moth moves its front wings the eye-shaped markings appear suddenly, and this frightens the attacker even more.

▲ With front wings closed

▲ With front wings spread apart

4

Aha! Food!

This bird has spotted a butterfly.

(ANSWER 2) Some butterflies have small eye-shaped markings on their wings. An attacker will think the markings are the butterfly's head and will peck at them. But since it hasn't really been pecked in the head, the butterfly can escape.

The bird pecks at the eye-shaped markings instead of the real eyes.

Even though its wing is torn the butterfly escapes by flying away.

Caterpillars with eye-shaped markings

Markings that look like eyes are found not only on adult butterflies and moths. Some caterpillars have them too. When an attacker appears the caterpillars curl up so that the eyelike markings appear. That generally frightens the attacker away.

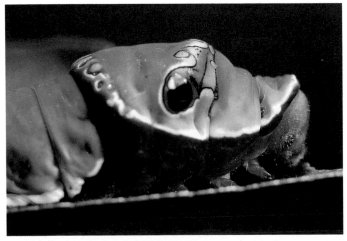

▲ **Black swallowtail caterpillar.** It has eyelike markings on the part of its body called the thorax.

▲ This upside-down one seems to have two eyes.

▲ This caterpillar looks like a snake.

● **To the Parent**

The eyelike markings on some butterflies and moths are thought to have two purposes. One is to frighten away attackers. The other is to present false eyes to an enemy to lure it away from the true eyes. Birds are scared off by the large eye-shaped markings, but they will aim their attacks at the smaller markings, which serve to divert their attention away from the real eyes.

❓ Why Does This Caterpillar Grow Horns?

ANSWER This is a swallowtail caterpillar. If something touches it or shakes the branch that it's on, the caterpillar puts out yellow horns that give off a bad smell. That's the way the swallowtail protects itself from enemies. Whatever is attacking the larva is frightened away by the awful-smelling horns that appear.

▲ The swallowtail caterpillar puts out horns that give off a bad smell.

The Secret of the Swallowtail Caterpillar's Body

The caterpillar is very different from an adult butterfly. Let's take a close look to see just how it's different.

The real eyes are very small, and there are six of them on either side of the head.

▲ **Eye-shaped markings.** They look like large eyes but really are markings on the body.

These holes are for breathing. Air goes in and out here.

There are pointed legs on the thorax. On the abdomen, or belly, are rounded legs with claws on the ends.

Tubes to digest leaves

Eyes

Urine is made here

Thread is made in this sac

It spins a thread and hooks its claws onto the thread so that it won't slip when it walks.

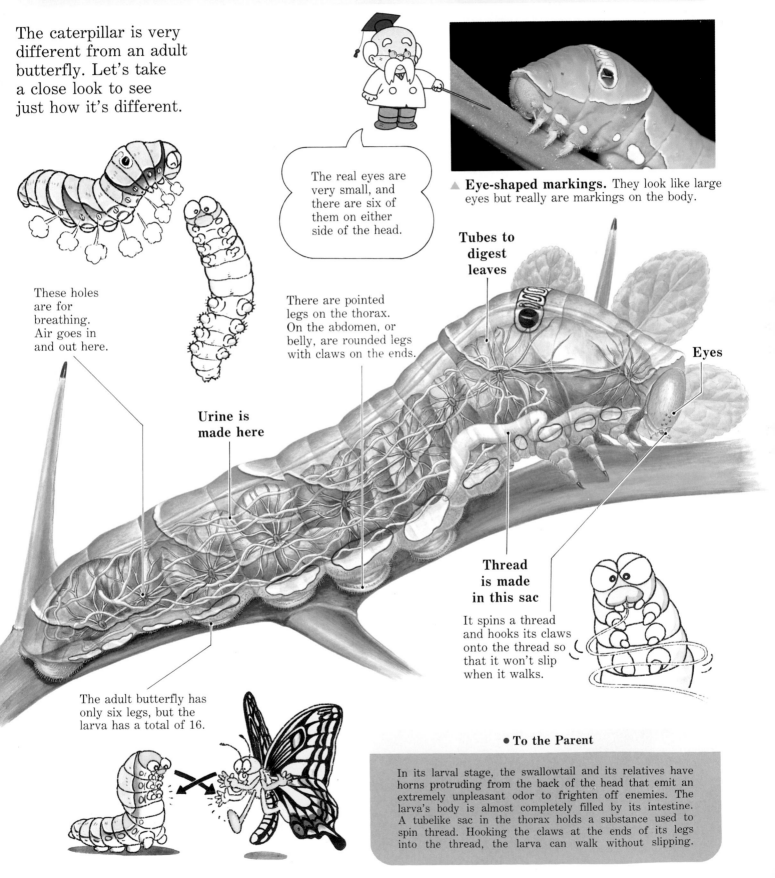

The adult butterfly has only six legs, but the larva has a total of 16.

● **To the Parent**

In its larval stage, the swallowtail and its relatives have horns protruding from the back of the head that emit an extremely unpleasant odor to frighten off enemies. The larva's body is almost completely filled by its intestine. A tubelike sac in the thorax holds a substance used to spin thread. Hooking the claws at the ends of its legs into the thread, the larva can walk without slipping.

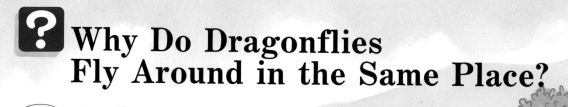

Why Do Dragonflies Fly Around in the Same Place?

ANSWER They are protecting their territory. The male silver dragonfly claims an area where the female can lay her eggs. Then he patrols that territory, and if any other males come into it he chases them away.

Female silver dragonfly

Male silver dragonfly

I'm with her!

I'll rest.

▲ **Male silver dragonfly.** It flies with its legs tucked in. The female dragonfly has a green chest.

❓ Why Do Some Bugs Stink?

ANSWER ▶ That awful smell protects them from their enemies. When a stinkbug is attacked it sprays liquid from holes in its body. The liquid turns into a mist that smells terrible. When other insects breathe in the mist their bodies begin to shiver and shake.

▲ **Protecting its young.** When a spider comes near, the stinkbug sprays out a smelly mist.

Spray holes

Liquid comes out of holes near the middle legs.

10

To warn other stinkbugs of danger. The smell lets the other bugs know that an enemy is near. If one of the bugs is attacked, the others will run away as fast as they can after they have smelled the warning spray.

Stinkbugs and skunks use an unpleasant smell for protection.

●To the Parent

Stinkbugs produce an odor so revolting it is hard to describe. The smell comes from a gland that secretes a liquid. Sprayed out through holes located where the middle legs join the body, the liquid becomes a mist with a foul smell that drives away enemies. The smell has no effect, however, on some attackers such as praying mantises, chickens or frogs. One kind of stinkbug, which lays its eggs on cedar and other needles, uses the spray to protect the larvae. And some of the bugs found living in colonies on arrowroot leaves use their smelly spray to warn other members of the colony of an attack.

❓ Why Do Cicadas Sing?

ANSWER The male cicadas are the ones that sing. They do it to attract mates. When a male is singing, not only females but other males gather around. Once the males and females have gathered, they find partners that suit them, then they mate.

Brown cicada

❓ How Do Cicadas Make Sounds?

They use special sound-making organs that are inside their stomach. The sounds are made by muscles and membranes on the bottom of the male cicada's stomach. When the muscles vibrate the membrane it makes a small sound, which becomes much larger after it echoes inside a space in the cicada's stomach.

Inside a cicada's stomach

Sound membrane

Space to make the sound louder

Muscles to vibrate the membrane

The sound becomes loud enough to hear after it echoes inside a space in the cicada's stomach.

Kaempfer cicada

Which way?

▲ **Kaempfer cicada.** The male sings when the female above starts to pay attention to him.

Making a toy cicada out of bamboo

Some Asian children make toy cicadas. They make a tiny drum from bamboo and paper. Then they put pine resin on a stick and attach the drum to it with string. When they twirl the toy the string rubs against the resin and makes a small sound. The string carries the sound to the drum, which makes it louder.

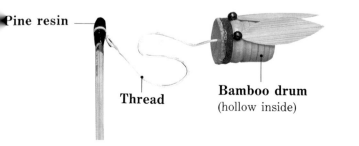

Pine resin

Thread

Bamboo drum
(hollow inside)

•To the Parent

Male cicadas produce different kinds of sounds. One is a congregational call that attracts both females and other males. Another sound is produced when the male approaches or courts a female. And yet another sound is heard when the cicada is in distress, as when it has been captured.

13

❓ Why Do Crickets Chirp?

ANSWER 1 Only the male crickets make sounds. In that way they're like cicadas. The cricket you see here makes three different kinds of chirping sounds. It uses one of those to keep other males out of its territory. The cricket uses a different chirping sound to call females.

ANSWER 2 When the male cricket is trying to attract a female, it uses another kind of sound. The male tries to make the female take a liking to him with his special chirping song.

ANSWER 3 These male crickets make yet another kind of chirping sound when they're fighting each other. As they chirp they butt their heads together. When one gives up and runs away, the noise stops.

How insects make their chirping sounds

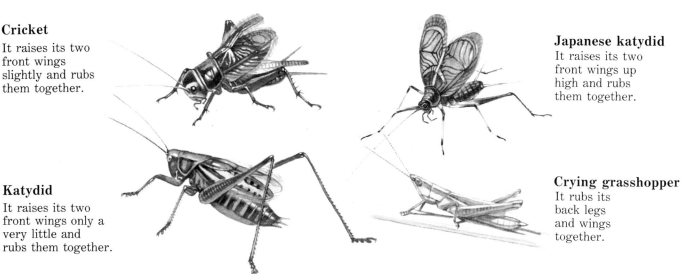

Cricket
It raises its two front wings slightly and rubs them together.

Katydid
It raises its two front wings only a very little and rubs them together.

Japanese katydid
It raises its two front wings up high and rubs them together.

Crying grasshopper
It rubs its back legs and wings together.

15

❓ Did You Know That Some Ants Steal Young Ants From Other Nests?

(ANSWER) Slave-maker ants keep black ants as slaves. The slave-maker ants raid black ants' nests and steal the unborn ants, which are called pupas. They take these back to their own nest, where the pupas become adult ants and spend their lives serving their captors.

Inside a slave-maker ant nest

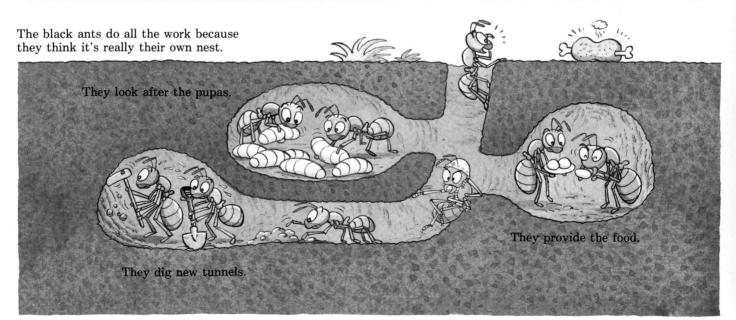

The black ants do all the work because they think it's really their own nest.

They look after the pupas.

They dig new tunnels.

They provide the food.

The body of a slave-maker ant

Because their jaws are so large, they can't eat without help. So they get black ants to feed them.

They use their strong jaws to hold and carry away the pupas when they raid a nest of black ants.

▲ **Face of a slave-maker ant**

● **To the Parent**

Slave-maker ants keep black ants in their nests and use them as servants. When enough of the black ants living in the slave-maker ants' nest have died off, an army of the latter goes out to raid a nest of black ants to steal pupas and cocoons and then take them back to their nests. When the black ants hatch in the other ants' nest, they think they are in their own nest, and they go to work right away.

? **What Does a Tumblebug Eat?**

(ANSWER) The tumblebug eats dung. This is the waste left by larger animals. It makes little balls of dung so that it can roll them to a place where it's safe to eat them.

Whenever they pick up the smell of dung, large numbers of tumblebugs come from all around.

They take small pieces from a lump of dung until they've formed a round ball.

▲ **Tumblebug rolling a ball of dung.** It uses its front legs to support its body and move along while it rolls the ball with its middle and back legs.

■ A tumblebug having a meal

The tumblebug has to watch out for enemies and competitors in places where dung is found.

They dig holes in the earth and eat their food underground.

▲ A yellow baboon is one of the tumblebug's enemies. The baboon breaks up pieces of dung and eats insects it finds.

■ Providing food for their young

The tumblebug buries a pear-shaped lump of dung in the ground and lays its eggs inside it. When the larvae hatch they will eat the dung.

▲ Eggs are laid in pear-shaped balls of dung. Here the surface has been scraped away to show the egg inside.

A chamber is dug 16 to 20 inches (40 to 50 cm) below ground, and balls of dung are laid on their side in the nest.

● To the Parent

Insects that live on the manure of animals are called dung beetles. One of these is the tumblebug, a beetle that feeds on herbivorous animals' dung, which it rolls into balls. The insect feeds on dungballs and lays its eggs in them. When the larvae hatch, they start feeding on the dung. In ancient Egypt the sacred scarab was a dung beetle and was worshipped as a symbol of the sun moving the earth.

How Do Spiders Spin Webs?

ANSWER In a spider's web some of the threads are sticky and some are not. The spider first spins the framework of the net with threads that aren't sticky and uses those as a foothold. Then it spins the rest of the web with threads that are extremely sticky.

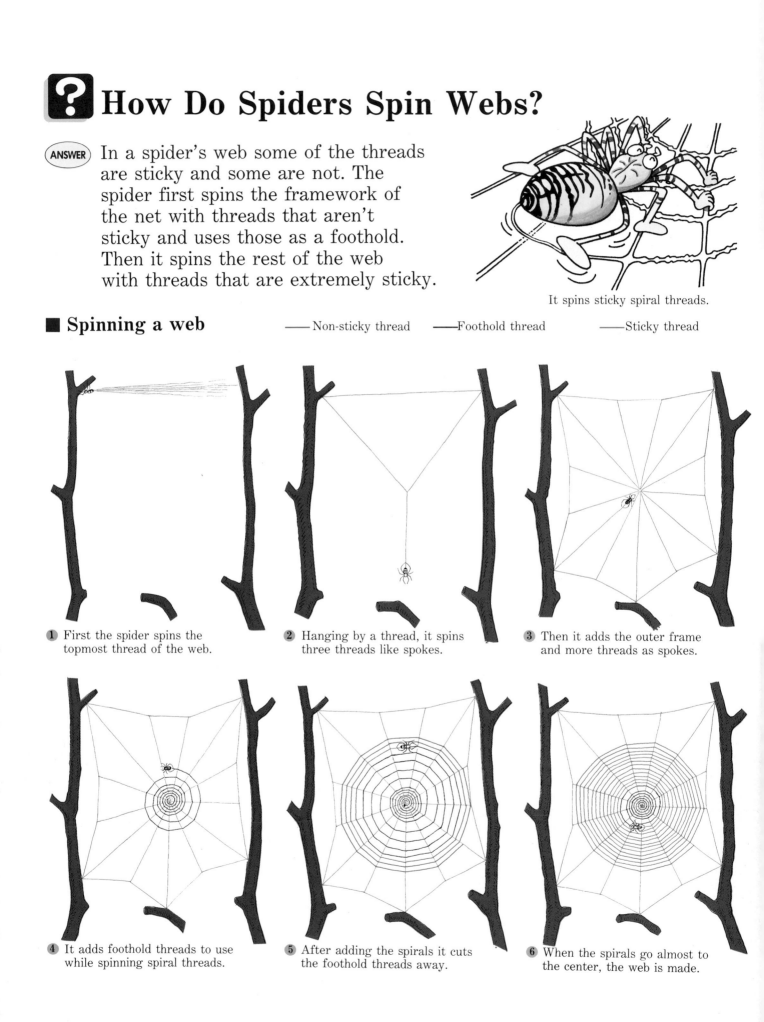

It spins sticky spiral threads.

■ Spinning a web

—— Non-sticky thread　——Foothold thread　——Sticky thread

❶ First the spider spins the topmost thread of the web.

❷ Hanging by a thread, it spins three threads like spokes.

❸ Then it adds the outer frame and more threads as spokes.

❹ It adds foothold threads to use while spinning spiral threads.

❺ After adding the spirals it cuts the foothold threads away.

❻ When the spirals go almost to the center, the web is made.

The center does not catch anything.

▲ **Web of a golden spider.** The spider waits in the center of the web, where the threads are not sticky.

Some of the webs that spiders spin

The bowl spider's web has lots of threads and looks like an upside-down bowl.

The fan spider spins a three-cornered web like an open fan.

The shelf spider spins a web that looks like a shelf inside bushes.

● **To the Parent**

When spiders begin a web they spin many threads into the wind until one is anchored. Then they cut the others and use the first one to start the frame. Threads for the frame, spokes and footholds are not sticky, but the spiral threads have a sticky substance on them to trap insects.

Where Is the Mouth of a Starfish?

ANSWER A starfish's mouth is on the underside of its body. The mouth is the opening in the center where the five arms meet. When a starfish wants to eat, its stomach comes out through the mouth, closes over the prey and digests it.

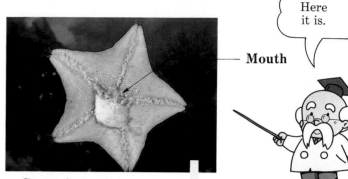

Mouth

Here it is.

▲ Capturing a fish

▲ **A starfish digesting a fish.** The light-colored stomach emerges from the mouth to digest the food.

And What Do Starfish Eat?

▲ A starfish eating a clam

Starfish eat fish, clams and other shellfish.

▲ Spider starfish eating tiny sea animals

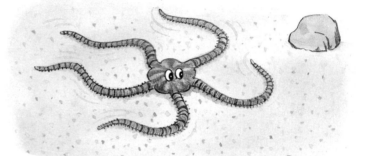

The spider starfish eats very small creatures that it finds on the sand or on rocks.

▲ Crown-of-thorns starfish eating coral

This one also eats small animals that form coral.

MINI-DATA

Starfish have thousands of tiny tubes that act like little feet. The starfish can attach those tubes to objects by suction. By tugging away at a closed shell for a long time they finally get it open, then eat the food.

The crown-of-thorns starfish has poisonous spikes.

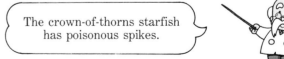

• To the Parent

The mouth of the starfish is located in the center of its underside. There are no teeth or tentacles in the mouth. Instead the starfish uses an unusual method of digestion in which it turns its stomach inside out, envelops the prey and digests it outside the body. A starfish has tubular feet with suction pads on the ends for attaching themselves. To eat a bivalve shellfish the starfish uses the suction feet to pull at the shell until it opens.

How Do Sea Anemones Catch Fish?

ANSWER The tentacles of a sea anemone have poison spines on them. When a fish touches one of the tentacles it gets stuck by a poison spine so that it cannot move. Then the anemone uses its tentacles to pull the fish in.

▲ A sea anemone catches a small fish.

The sea anemone spreads out its tentacles and waits for a fish to come along.

When a fish touches the tentacles, poison spines come out and touch the fish.
The poison makes the fish unable to move.

When the fish stops moving, the anemone pulls it inside its body and digests it.

Secret of the poison spines

The poison spines are located in small sacs in the tentacles.
When something disturbs them they pop out suddenly.

Like a blowpipe!

When it can't eat any more it pushes the leftovers outside.

24

Then Why Doesn't the Anemone Fish Get Hurt?

The anemone fish lives all its life very near the poisonous sea anemone. The fish is all right even when it bumps against the tentacles. The body of the fish is covered with a film that protects it against the anemone's poison spines.

The body of the anemone fish is covered with a layer of film.

▲ The anemone fish lives around the sea anemone.

The poison spines of the sea anemone can't pass through the layer of film, so the anemone fish is safe.

MINI-DATA

What would happen if all of the film were wiped off the anemone fish's body? If that happened it would lose its protection and be just like other fish. The poison spines would sting it and the sea anemone would eat it.

The anemone fish gets away from its attackers by hiding in the safety of the sea anemone's tentacles.

●To the Parent

The sea anemone and jellyfish are members of the phylum Cnidaria and are characterized by stinging cells called cnidocysts. If stimulated, as when brushed against by a fish, a stinging nettle coiled inside the cnidocyst pops out, pierces the offender's skin and injects a poison that is paralyzing. The immobilized fish is then ingested.

Why Do Salmon Return to Where They Were Born?

(ANSWER) Salmon spend most of their life in the ocean, but they return to the river where they were born when it's time to lay eggs. Salmon can remember the smell of the river they originally came from. Once they find it, they swim up it and spawn.

Here's mine.

Which one is mine?

A salmon jumps in the mouth of a river. Once their bodies are used to the fresh water they start upstream.

How Can They Find Their Way in the Ocean?

A salmon uses smell as its guide to find the river where it was born, once it gets near enough to the smell of that river. But we still don't know how a salmon can tell which direction to go when it's too far out at sea to pick up the smell of the river. Some people think the position of the sun tells the salmon which way to go. Others say the fish may have something in its body that works like a magnet.

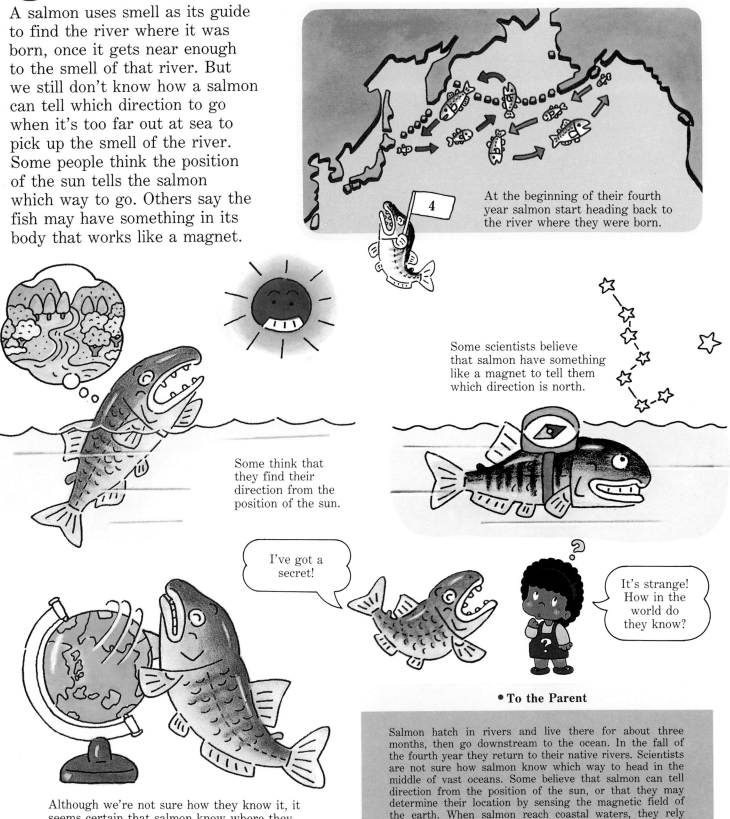

At the beginning of their fourth year salmon start heading back to the river where they were born.

Some scientists believe that salmon have something like a magnet to tell them which direction is north.

Some think that they find their direction from the position of the sun.

I've got a secret!

It's strange! How in the world do they know?

Although we're not sure how they know it, it seems certain that salmon know where they are even in the middle of the huge ocean.

● To the Parent

Salmon hatch in rivers and live there for about three months, then go downstream to the ocean. In the fall of the fourth year they return to their native rivers. Scientists are not sure how salmon know which way to head in the middle of vast oceans. Some believe that salmon can tell direction from the position of the sun, or that they may determine their location by sensing the magnetic field of the earth. When salmon reach coastal waters, they rely on memory to detect the smell of their river of origin.

Why Do Angler Fish Have Lights?

ANSWER 1 To catch small fish to eat. They are attracted by the lights at the end of that "fishing rod" that sticks out of the forehead of the angler fish.

ANSWER 2 To protect itself from enemies. If an enemy approaches, the fish shoots a glowing liquid out of its fishing rod. That stuns the attacker.

Boy! Did he get a surprise!

Do Other Deep-Sea Fish Have Lights?

Some deep-sea fish have a stomach that glows. The sea is lighter at the surface, so enemies attacking from below can't see them easily.

The part of the fish that glows depends on what kind of fish it is. In the deep, dark parts of the ocean the glowing lights help to identify other fish of the same species.

Fish of the same species glow in the same way.

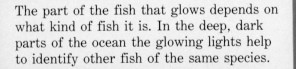

❓ Did You Know That Some Fish Build Nests Like Bird Nests?

(ANSWER) The stickleback uses the stalks and roots of water plants to make a round nest that looks just like some birds' nests. The male stickleback builds the nest and then invites a female into it. The female enters the nest, lays her eggs and swims away. The male then looks after the eggs until they hatch into young fish, called fry. He also looks after the fry until they're old enough to swim away on their own.

That fish's nest is like a bird's nest.

■ The stickleback nest and the male's duties

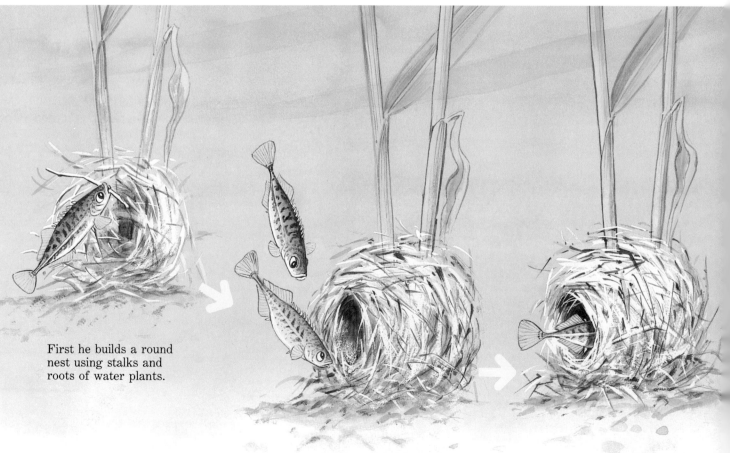

First he builds a round nest using stalks and roots of water plants.

When the nest is finished, he brings a female back to it to get her to lay her eggs there.

The female goes into the nest and lays her eggs inside it.

■ On guard

The stickleback's nest of branches and plants is complete. There are eggs inside the nest.

Male stickleback▶
protecting its nest
Inset: the eggs▶

If another male or an enemy approaches, the nest builder chases it away.

Finally the eggs hatch, and the fry swim around close to the nest.

● To the Parent

Most sticklebacks, sometimes called tittlebacks, have nine spines along the back. In spring and early summer the male prepares for the mating season by building a nest a short distance above the river bed or sea bottom. The female lays 20 to 30 eggs in the nest at one time. The male has a very strong territorial instinct and does not allow enemies or rival males to approach his nest.

How Do Archerfish Catch Prey?

ANSWER Archerfish catch insects by shooting them with water. They can make their mouth into the shape of a tube and shoot water out of it in a powerful jet, much like a water pistol.

An archerfish shoots water at a caterpillar on a leaf.

Watch out, caterpillar!

How an Archerfish Catches Its Dinner

First it spots a juicy caterpillar and takes aim.

Then it shoots a jet of water from its mouth.

The caterpillar falls into the water and is eaten.

●To the Parent

The archerfish lives in river mouths and along coasts in Southeast Asia. Because of its ability to shoot a jet of water to knock down insects or worms above the water's surface, it is a popular exhibit in aquariums. In its upper jaw is a narrow groove that the fish, by using its tongue, can turn into a tube. It then uses its gill flaps to pressurize the water and shoot it out through its mouth. It has excellent aim and rarely misses its prey.

❓ Do Electric Eels Really Make Electricity?

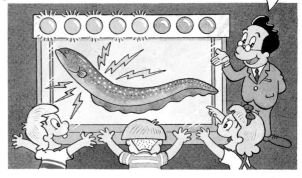

It turns on all these lights.

ANSWER Yes, they certainly do! Their bodies can produce a very strong jolt of electricity. In some aquariums you can see demonstrations of how electric eels produce enough power to turn lights on. They can shock whatever is swimming in the water around them.

I'd better watch out. I don't want to get shocked.

▲ **An electric eel.** It is eight feet (2.4 m) long and lives in rivers in South America.

Why Does It Produce Electricity?

The electric eel uses electricity as a weapon to catch food and to protect itself from its enemies. It can produce a jolt of electricity strong enough to give a severe shock to anything nearby. The eel also gives off a lower amount of electricity all the time, using it like radar to detect the underwater objects in its surroundings.

It protects itself from enemies by giving them a strong shock.

It paralyzes small fish with a shock and then eats them.

The electric eel can't see very well, so it uses electricity to help it avoid obstacles in the water.

Other fish that produce electricity

▲ **Electric catfish.** It lives in African rivers and ponds.

▲ **Electric ray.** It lives in the oceans.

●**To the Parent**

The electric eel produces electricity in modified muscle tissue activated by nerves. It can emit a momentary burst of electricity as high as 650 volts, which can stun large animals. In addition to these strong emissions used to attack prey and ward off enemies, a weaker electrical discharge is used to learn about the eel's surroundings.

How Do Frogs and Toads Catch Food With Their Tongues?

(ANSWER) Their tongue is very sticky, and they can shoot it out a long, long way. If they see an insect that they want, they shoot out their long tongue and catch it.

▲ A toad finds something to eat.

▲ A toad catches an insect by rolling up its tongue and then eats the insect stuck at the end of it.

36

A Frog Will Try to Catch Anything That Moves

Frogs like to eat insects that are living. If they see something that's moving and looks as if it will fit inside their mouth, they'll try to catch it. Sometimes, though, they make a mistake and swallow the wrong thing.

Frogs will catch only things that are moving.

If an insect doesn't move, the frog won't touch it.

Ha! I'll fool him. I'll just play dead.

MINI-DATA

Sometimes a frog will attack a blade of grass waving in the wind because it thinks the grass is something to eat. It might attack a stalk of a river fern that grows near water. If three or four tips on the stalk were shaken in front of a frog, the frog would think it was something to eat and try to catch it.

■ A frog that's made a mistake

▲ A leopard frog catches a crawfish.

▲ The frog is surprised to have its tongue pinched by the crawfish's claw, and it spits the crawfish out.

● To the Parent

When a frog spots a moving insect that it wants to eat, it quickly leaps forward and at the same time opens its large mouth and flicks out its tongue. On the end of the tongue of most types of frogs are two small protrusions which are wrapped around the prey being captured. Most frogs eat insects and worms. Some larger species of frogs, however, eat small rodents and other vertebrates.

❓ Why Does a Lizard's Tail Break Off?

ANSWER ◆ A lizard's tail breaks very easily. If an enemy catches it, the tail breaks off and the lizard can get away.

■ The breaking point

The lizard's tail can break off anywhere near its rear end.

It can break anywhere after this point.

▲ **A severed tail**
It's not very painful.

ANSWER 2 The tail jerks and twitches for a while after it has broken off. It gets the attention of an attacker, like a cat, and that gives the lizard time to escape to a safer place.

● **To the Parent**

When a lizard is caught by the tail, the tail breaks off at the point where pressure is applied to it. This self-amputation, called autotomy, allows the lizard to escape. The severed tail continues to move, diverting the attacker's attention while the lizard gets away. A new tail begins growing immediately and reaches normal size within a few months.

Now's your chance to get away, while the cat's looking at the tail.

 # What Happens After the Tail Breaks Off?

A new tail grows in place of the old one. This is called regeneration.

▲ **Lizard with its original tail.** If the tail has never been broken off, it might be very long.

▲ **Lizard with a regenerated tail.** A new tail has grown but it's rather short and has a strange shape.

? Did You Know That One Lizard Can Run on Water?

(ANSWER) The basilisk lizard can run across the water. It takes a step with its left foot before the right one can sink, then it takes the next step with its right foot before the left foot sinks. The lizard doesn't sink because its body is very light and because it spreads the toes of its back feet extremely wide to keep them from sinking.

The secret's here on the bottom.

▲ Scales spread between the toes of the back feet.

When the basilisk runs on the water it has to move very quickly to keep from sinking.

● To the Parent

The basilisk lizard will run on the surface of the water to escape from an enemy. The basilisk is able to move on top of the water because it can spread the toes of its hind feet. When the surface area of the feet is extended, there is increased surface tension on the water, which supports the lizard as it moves quickly. The basilisk can also swim, however, and can remain submerged for long periods.

A basilisk races over ▶ the surface, splashing water as it goes.

40

❓ Why Do Turtles Come Up on Land?

ANSWER If you go to visit a pond or stream on a warm, sunny day you may find turtles that have come up onto land. Sometimes they climb onto rocks and fallen trees. They do this to sunbathe so they can dry out their shells.

They look heavy.

▲ **Turtles drying their shells**

? Why Do They Want to Dry Their Shells?

To make them harder and stronger. The shells get soft and weak if they don't dry out from time to time.

To get rid of the plants or animals that have become attached to their bodies.

To warm their bodies after the chill of the water.

Don't give them sunstroke
Turtles need sunlight. But if you keep turtles in an aquarium, be sure they aren't in the sun too long on sunny days. If the water gets too warm the turtles won't feel well.

• **To the Parent**

Turtles need sunlight so that their bodies will produce enough vitamin D to keep their shells and bones from becoming weak. Turtles also need sunlight to regulate their temperature. Because they are cold-blooded, their body temperature is strongly affected by temperatures around them. In cold water too long, they become sluggish from the low temperatures and need to sunbathe to warm up. Sunning also helps to get rid of parasites and algae.

? Why Do Sea Turtles Leave the Water To Lay Their Eggs?

ANSWER They can't get oxygen from the water the way fish can. If the sea turtle's eggs hatched in the water the baby turtles would drown right away. In fact if a sea turtle laid her eggs in the sea, they would go bad even before they could hatch. That would happen because even the eggs need air. And that's why the sea turtles leave the water to lay their eggs.

This is awful! I can't breathe!

■ Red sea turtle laying her eggs

Look at all those eggs!

When it's time for the sea turtle to lay her eggs she leaves the water and crawls up onto the beach. She digs a hole in the sand, and there she lays her eggs.

The female sea turtle digs a hole about 16 inches (40 cm) deep and lays about 120 eggs.

She digs the hole with her back legs.

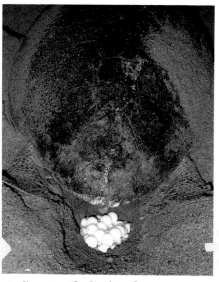

▲ **Sea turtle laying her eggs**

When she has finished she uses her back legs to fill up the hole with sand and cover the eggs.

The Turtle's Life Cycle

The baby turtles that have just hatched begin to move toward the sea as soon as they can crawl out of the nest. The sea is where they will grow up. When the females are grown and ready to lay eggs themselves they will return to the beach.

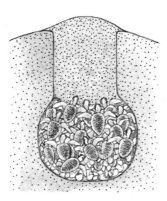

The eggs hatch after about two months.

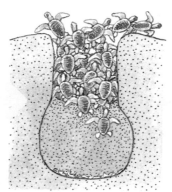

The baby turtles all leave the nest together.

Their enemies are sea gulls and crabs.

▲ Baby turtles crawl toward the sea. They start for the water as soon as they come out of the nest.

The turtles grow into adults in warm ocean waters. When it's time to lay eggs they return to land.

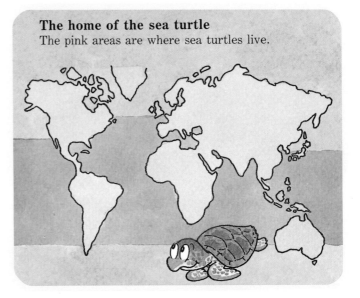

The home of the sea turtle
The pink areas are where sea turtles live.

● **To the Parent**

Sea turtles are air-breathing reptiles. If their eggs hatched under water the baby turtles would drown. Actually, however, they could not hatch there, because the eggs must breathe through their shells. Also there would not be enough heat for them to develop under water. For these reasons the sea turtle must come up onto dry land to lay its eggs.

Why Do Cranes Stand on One Leg?

(ANSWER) A crane's body is covered almost all over with feathers to keep it warm. But the crane loses heat through its legs because there are no feathers on them. To save as much heat as it can, the crane stands on only one leg and tucks the other one up against its body.

I get cold if I use both feet.

It doesn't fall down

If people try to stand on only one leg with their eyes closed they soon fall down. But cranes can even go to sleep while standing on one leg. They stand on one leg all night long and it doesn't bother them a bit.

Cranes sleep while standing in an icy river in the winter.

● **To the Parent**

Most birds rest their breast on the ground or a tree branch and tuck their head under their wing when they sleep. Cranes and some other water birds often sleep standing in water. They stand on only one leg so that they can reduce loss of body heat as much as possible.

Did You Know That Some Birds' Babies Are Raised by Another Bird?

ANSWER Some birds don't raise their own babies. They have found a way to get other birds to do the work for them. Cuckoos, for instance, lay eggs in reed warblers' nests. When the cuckoo chick hatches, the reed warbler feeds it and takes care of it.

The cuckoo chick grows larger than the reed warbler.

The cuckoo waits for a chance to lay her eggs.

▲ **Adult cuckoo**

▲ Even when the warbler's there the cuckoo shoves its eggs out.

The cuckoo waits until the warbler is away from the nest, then moves in and lays an egg.

The cuckoo eats one of the warbler's eggs and replaces it by laying one of its own eggs.

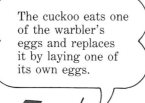

▲ The cuckoo's egg is a little larger than the others.

▲ The cuckoo chick that's just hatched shoves all the reed warbler's eggs out of the nest.

▲ The young cuckoo gets all the food, so it grows larger than its foster parents.

Birds raised by others

Here are some birds that get
other birds to raise their young.

Paradise whydah

Honey guide

Common cuckoo

Chinese hawk cuckoo

●To the Parent

One of the most unusual phenomena in the animal world
is the parasitic instinct of some birds that do not
build nests of their own but lay their eggs in other
birds' nests to be taken care of. The cuckoo is one of
these. Its chick hatches before the other eggs in the
nest and shoves the other eggs out. This instinctive action
occurs even when the foster parents are in the nest.

❓ Why Do Some Birds Migrate?

(ANSWER) We say that birds migrate when they leave one area and fly to another. They may migrate because a place becomes too cold for them or there's no longer enough food. When the seasons change and there's more food the birds fly back to their first homes.

When the place they were born gets too cold birds begin migrating.

Back in their birthplace again, they build nests and raise their young.

The migrating birds leave home and fly south.

After spending the winter in the south, the migrating birds fly back to their homes in the north.

In the south birds find much warmer weather and more food than in the places they left behind.

When the seasons change and the place they came from is warm again, the birds begin their return migration.

Note: The arrows on the map are only symbolic representations of the north-south routes that migrating birds usually follow.

?? How Far Do Birds Travel When They Migrate?

Some birds fly much farther than others. The bird that's best known for migrating long distances is the arctic tern. When winter approaches the tern leaves its birthplace near the North Pole and migrates to Antarctica, almost all the way to the South Pole.

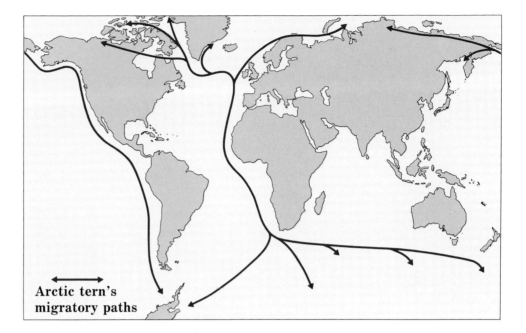

Arctic tern's migratory paths

Cranes that cross the Himalayas

▲ Cranes passing over Mt. Manaslu in the Himalayas

Cranes that migrate from Siberia to India have to cross the Himalayas, the world's highest mountains. They have to fly very high, where there's little oxygen.

● To the Parent

Migration refers to the annual round trip that birds make in response to seasonal changes in their food supply. Almost half of the world's birds migrate. The greatest of these travelers is the arctic tern, which nests in the northern polar regions. During the eight months in which the tern is not nesting its migratory flight to and from Antarctica may cover nearly 24,000 miles (38,623 km).

❓ Why Does the Male Bowerbird Decorate Its Nest So Carefully?

ANSWER The male bowerbird gathers brush to build a nest, called a bower. He decorates his home with whatever he can find. He will mate with a female in the bower, but first he has to attract her by having a beautiful bower. That's why he spends a lot of time building and decorating it.

▲ Male bowerbird

Come and be my mate.

▲ The bowerbird builds his bower on the ground and decorates it with anything colorful that he can find.

52

▲ When the male has finished decorating his bower, here using plastic and other things, he invites a female in.

▲ The female's colors are different.

■ The courtship

The male performs a mating dance in front of his bower as he tries to attract the female.

● To the Parent

The male of various species of bowerbirds, found in Australia and New Guinea, builds and decorates a structure called a bower to attract a female. The male bowerbird will collect feathers, plastic and various other colorful objects to decorate its bower. When the bower is finished the male calls a female and attempts to attract her favor by dancing in front of the bower and pointing out its fine features with his beak. If the female is impressed, she enters the bower and mates with its builder. After they mate the female goes away and builds her own nest, in which she lays her eggs.

Why Does This Bird Build a Big Mound?

ANSWER The mallee fowl builds a mound so that its eggs will hatch. The male makes a very large mound out of dead leaves, sand and earth. Then the female lays eggs in the mound. As the leaves rot they produce heat, keeping the eggs warm so they will hatch.

Inside view of the mound

Leaves that were gathered and put into the mallee's mound four or five months ago have already rotted.

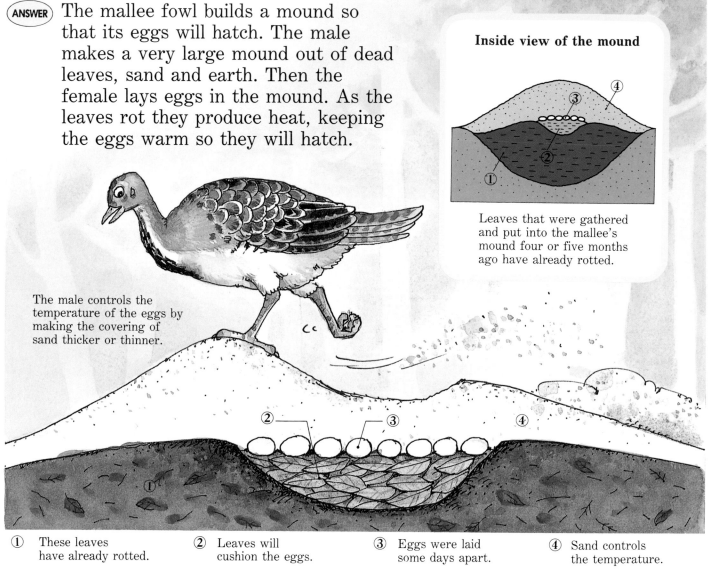

The male controls the temperature of the eggs by making the covering of sand thicker or thinner.

① These leaves have already rotted.

② Leaves will cushion the eggs.

③ Eggs were laid some days apart.

④ Sand controls the temperature.

■ The mallee fowl's eggs hatch

The male digs a hole in the rotted leaves and then adds some new leaves, on which the female begins laying eggs.

The male covers the eggs with sand or earth so that the heat won't escape. The mound grows higher and higher.

▲ **Red mallee fowl.** Shown here in the inset circle, it has built its mound in the forest.

By adjusting the thickness of the layer of sand the male is able to keep the mound at a constant temperature.

Why Do a Chipmunk's Cheeks Puff Out?

ANSWER A chipmunk can puff out its cheeks to hold lots of acorns and other things it likes to eat.
That's the way the chipmunk carries its food around.

That's convenient.

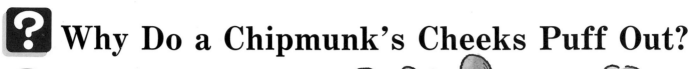

■ Cheek pouches

The chipmunk's cheeks are like a basket for holding things.
The cheeks form pouches, which can be stuffed full of food.

▲ When the pouches are empty

▲ When the pouches are full

Where Do They Take the Acorns?

The chipmunks carry the acorns to their burrow or to places near the burrow. Then they dig holes and bury them. The acorns are what the chipmunk eats while it rests in its burrow in the winter.

When winter comes and snow falls they won't be able to find any food. But they can eat the acorns they've stored up during the autumn.

With its cheek pouches full of acorns, the chipmunk digs a hole.

It stores the nuts in a hole so that other animals won't get them.

The chipmunk carefully fills the hole and then pats the earth down with its paws.

■ The winter burrow

When winter comes the chipmunk holes up in its burrow under the ground. It sleeps most of the time, but once in a while it wakes up and eats some of the acorns that it has stored away for the long cold winter.

Acorns stored in holes dug near the burrow

Chipmunk holed up for winter

Acorns stored in the burrow

●To the Parent

A chipmunk can hold two acorns in each of its cheek pouches. The pouches are formed by sacs made of folds of skin on either side of the throat. Not only chipmunks but hamsters, pocket gophers and some monkeys have cheek pouches. Chipmunks use their pouches to carry food to places where they will store it as they prepare for hibernation. They also use them for taking food to their young and for carrying pieces of wood with which to line their burrows.

❓ Did You Know That Prairie Dogs Build Their Own Town?

(ANSWER) Families of prairie dogs burrow in the ground to make tunnels and nests. Since many families burrow in the same area, they build what looks like a large town of prairie dogs.

A town with a very good view

Prairie dogs eat all the grass near their burrows so that they'll have a much better view of what's around them.

With all the grass removed the guards can spot coyotes or any other enemies that might come near their home.

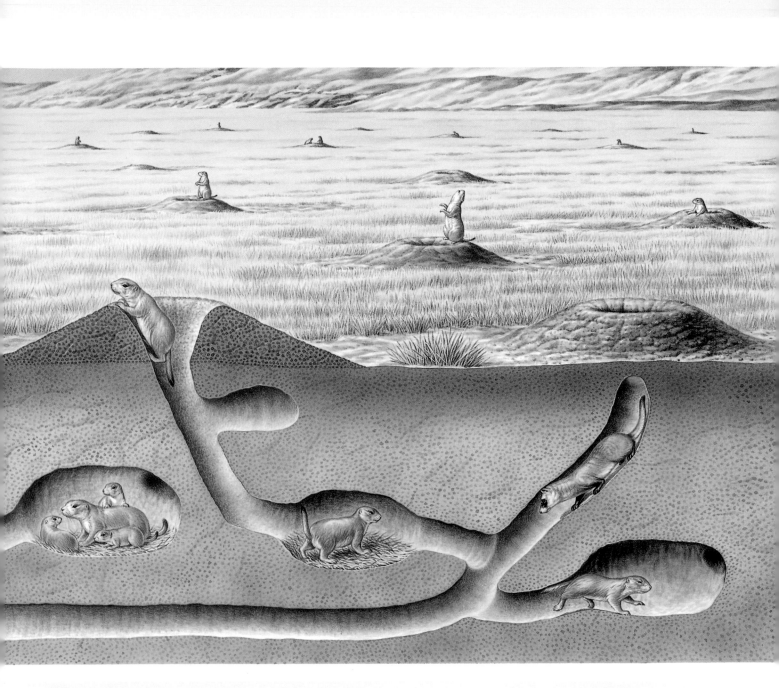

The prairie dog's real enemy

The badger preys on prairie dogs but cannot go farther than the opening of the burrow. But a weasel is thin enough to get into the burrow and attack.

● To the Parent

Prairie dogs are small burrowing rodents whose call is something like a dog barking. A family of prairie dogs usually is made up of a male, several females and a number of young. Such a family is known as a coterie, and a number of coteries close together form a town. Some towns may cover as much as 160 acres (65 ha). Prairie dogs eat the grass, especially any tall grass, in the vicinity of their burrow entrances. This eliminates all cover for predators, which can then be spotted in time for the prairie dogs to escape to the safety of their burrows. The prairie dogs' greatest enemy is the black-footed weasel, which is thin enough to get inside their burrows and attack them.

？ Why Do Bats Hang Upside Down?

ANSWER A bat's body is well suited to flying. The back legs are very thin. They are connected by a thin skin, called a membrane, that helps the bat fly. But the thin legs and the membrane make it hard for the bat to stand. That's why you always see bats hanging upside down.

▲ This mother bat and baby hang upside down.

The bat's wings have the same kind of bone structure as a person's hands. The legs are thin and have a membrane to help them fly. At the ends of a bat's legs there are claws.

You'll see when you compare the places that have the same numbers.

■ A bat's body
A bat's wing and a person's hand have the same number of fingers.

Bat wing ▶

Human hand ▶

Back leg. It is weak and thin.

Toes. They have claws at the end.

■ It's easy to fly from a high place

A bat can fly off whenever it wants if it's hanging upside down.

But it's much harder to take off from the ground.

One thing it doesn't do upside down!

Because its back legs are so thin and weak, a bat can't stand up.

❓ But How Do They Go to the Toilet?

The bat pulls itself up so that its rear end is pointing downward.

It uses its claws to pull itself upright.

Once the bat waste drops is turned upright between its legs.

● **To the Parent**

Bats are mammals that have wings and can fly. A bird's wing has feathers, but the bat's wing is formed from a thin membrane supported by long finger bones, or digits, of the forelegs. Another membrane extends between the tail and the hind legs to help the bat to fly. The animal's body is well suited to flying but not to walking or running.

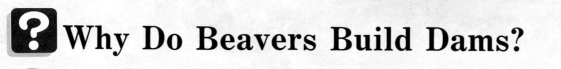

Why Do Beavers Build Dams?

(ANSWER) Beavers build a dam to stop up a river and form a pond. When a lot of water has backed up in the pond they build nests that look like small islands. With nests in the middle of the pond, beavers are safe from their enemies.

The entrance to the nest is hidden under the water's surface.

Beaver nest

Entrance

How the dam and nest are built

The beaver begins by building a dam of branches and mud in a stream. Water backs up behind the dam.

The beaver also uses branches and mud to build its nest out in the pond that's forming behind the dam.

Dam

Food stored for winter

■ A beaver cuts down a tree

A beaver has very strong teeth. It can cut down even a large tree by gnawing away at it.

It gnaws branches off the fallen tree, carries them to the pond and uses them to make its nest and dam.

The beaver eats some of the bark and leaves and stores some of it to eat when winter comes.

When the nest is finished and the pond has risen, the entrance is well hidden under the surface of the water.

● **To the Parent**

Beavers live near the water in the sub-arctic forests of North America and near the Elbe and Rhone rivers of Europe. Trees like the poplar and birch are sources of food and building materials for the beaver. The animal constructs dams of logs, branches and mud to arrest the flow of rivers so that a pond will be formed. In the pond the beaver builds a lodge that can be entered only from below the water. The depth of the water is regulated to conceal the entrance without covering the lodge's floor.

? **What Do Foxes Use Their Tails For?**

ANSWER A mother fox uses her tail as a signal for her pups to follow. The tip of a fox's tail is white. When the mother fox raises her tail it's very easy for the small foxes to see it. They can follow her easily without getting lost.

■ Animal tail signals

Golden cat. The fur on the bottom part of the golden cat's tail is white, and that makes it easy to see even in the dark.

Deer. When a deer raises its tail it shows white fur, which is very easy to see.

ANSWER 2 The fox uses its tail to help keep its balance when it's running and has to make a sharp turn. It also uses that bushy tail the way we would use a scarf, to wrap itself up and keep warm in the cold weather.

He's gone to sleep.

In cold weather the fox curls up and covers its face with its tail. This keeps heat from escaping, so the fox stays warm.

A running fox uses its tail for balance when making a sharp turn. That way its body won't tip over too far and it can make a smooth turn.

Wart hog. The mother and young wart hog hold their long tails straight up when they run.

MINI-DATA

Other animals that have their own scarf

Dormouse

Chipmunk

Chipmunks and dormice also use their tails as scarfs to keep warm when they're asleep.

● **To the Parent**

Some animals use their tail as a signaling device so that members of a herd or a mother and its young will not get separated. The tail often has white fur on it so that it can be seen easily even in thick underbrush or in the dark. Animals that have to chase nimble prey use their tail to help keep their balance when they suddenly change direction. In the winter, when its fur grows thicker, an animal uses its tail like a muffler to keep itself warm.

? How Do Sea Otters Open Seashells?

ANSWER The sea otter turns over onto its back, places a rock on its stomach and then breaks a seashell on the rock. Even the hardest shell will break if it's banged against the rock over and over again. Because it knows how to use rocks as tools the sea otter is able to eat shellfish.

Breaking a shell
The otter brings the shell down with a splash.

■ Catching its food

It digs in the sandy sea bottom until it finds a shellfish.

It uses a rock to break an abalone loose from a ledge it is clinging to.

■ Picking up a rock

Holding the shell under its flipper it swims to the surface with the rock.

Animals That Use Tools

Most animals and birds don't use tools, but there are some that do.

A chimpanzee sticks a straw into a termite nest and then eats the termites that cling to the straw.

When an Egyptian vulture wants to eat an ostrich egg it drops a rock on the egg to break it.

Wow! That looks hard!

■ Using its stomach as a table

After it has broken the shell open, the otter uses its stomach as a table and eats the meat inside the shell.

A woodpecker finch uses a cactus spine or a small twig to pick small insects out of a tree.

? What Do Deer Use Their Antlers For?

ANSWER Only the males have antlers. As the mating season gets closer, males lock horns and push each other around. They compete this way to show which one is stronger. The one that defeats the other gets to mate with a female.

The males lock horns and do battle.

How the antlers change

The antlers grow differently each year. In winter the antlers drop off at the roots but in spring they begin to grow back, covered with a soft skin like velvet. As spring turns to summer the antlers grow larger. In autumn the skin drops off and the deer has a strong, hard set of antlers with sharp points.

Spring

68

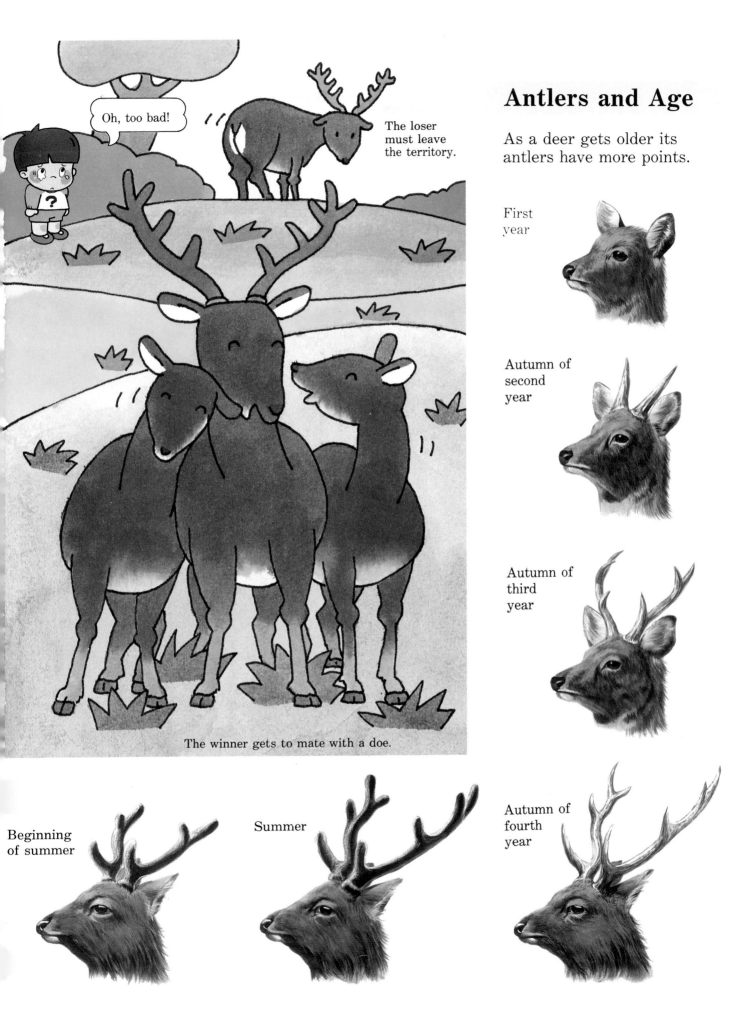

Oh, too bad!

The loser must leave the territory.

The winner gets to mate with a doe.

Antlers and Age

As a deer gets older its antlers have more points.

First year

Autumn of second year

Autumn of third year

Autumn of fourth year

Beginning of summer

Summer

Why Does a Hare's Fur Change Color?

ANSWER Many hares have fur that's brown in summer but white in winter. Snow falls in winter and everything is covered in white. With white fur it's easier for a hare to hide from its enemies. In summer it's easier for the hare to hide if it has brown fur. And that's the reason that the coat changes color.

Summer

Winter

■ How the hare's coat changes color

From summer to the middle of autumn its coat is brown.

The hare has both a summer coat and a winter coat.

About mid-autumn the hare starts losing its brown fur and growing white fur to replace it.

By winter the hare's coat is completely white except for the tips of its ears, which are always black.

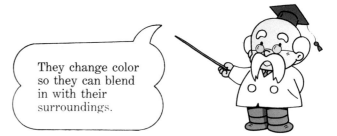

They change color so they can blend in with their surroundings.

The Secret of White Fur

Fur looks white because each hair is hollow. This kind of fur keeps the hare warm in winter.

Brrrrr!

I'm fine.

▲ **Snow hares.** Their coats are exactly the same color as the snow.

Brown hair isn't hollow at the center. It lets body heat escape much faster.

Hollow hair has air inside it, and that makes it harder for body heat to escape.

Animals that turn white in winter

Winter

Summer

Ermine

Summer

Winter

Pygmy weasel

Summer

Winter

Ptarmigan

● **To the Parent**

Hares living in colder areas have white fur in the winter and darker, usually grayish brown, fur in the summer. In warmer parts of the world hares are usually gray brown all year round. The winter coat appears white because each hair becomes hollow and fills with air. With air filling its center the hair reflects light and also provides insulation that conserves heat and keeps the animal warm.

Do Bears Really Sleep All Winter Long?

ANSWER Bears sleep through most of the winter in protected places such as caves, hollow trees, or holes that they dig beneath trees. But they may wake up if disturbed. On mild winter days, they will even come out of their warm dens to look for food.

Looks like he's comfortable!

How Bears Sleep Through the Winter

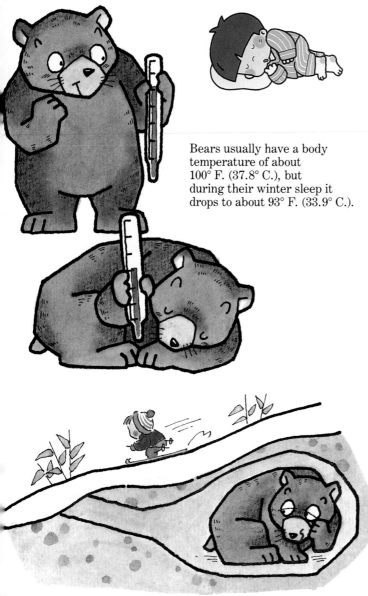

Bears usually have a body temperature of about 100° F. (37.8° C.), but during their winter sleep it drops to about 93° F. (33.9° C.).

▲ **A sleepy bear.** As the weather warms up in March, the bear wakes up and comes out of its den.

The female gives birth to cubs in her winter den. She usually has twins.

Bears don't sleep very soundly. If they're disturbed by a noise, they may wake up.

Many people say bears "hibernate" during the winter. But they don't—they just fall into a deep sleep. When an animal really hibernates, the way a chipmunk does, its body temperature drops very low and it doesn't breathe very much.

● **To the Parent**

In hibernation an animal's body temperature drops to the level of the surrounding temperature and the animal becomes almost completely inactive. Bears are not true hibernators. More precisely, they become dormant in the winter. As they sleep their body temperature seldom goes below 88° F. (31.1° C.). They may occasionally wake up and move about, and the females nurse their cubs.

? Why Do Orangutans Have Long Arms?

ANSWER Orangutans spend most of their life
in the trees of tropical forests.
They seldom come down to the ground.
As they move around in the trees they
hold on to the branches. With their
long arms it's easy for them to move
from one branch to the next. Their
long arms also help them reach for
the seeds and nuts they like to eat.

Down here I have to walk.

Life in the Trees

The gibbon uses its long arms to move rapidly through the treetops. It moves rapidly, one hand over the other.

The spider monkey uses not only its long arms and legs but its very long tail as it swings quickly from tree to tree.

● **To the Parent**

The orangutan is one of the anthropoid, or humanoid, apes and is found on the islands of Borneo and Sumatra in Southeast Asia. It normally lives in trees, but on the rare occasions when it comes down to the ground it walks on all fours. The orangutan is distinguished by the way it clenches its hind feet into fists as it walks. The chimpanzee and gorilla are also anthropoid apes, but they live primarily on the ground and keep their hind feet flat when they walk. Like orangutans, most apes and monkeys that live and move about freely in the trees have long arms to help them grasp branches.

Can Dolphins Talk?

ANSWER Dolphins constantly cry out to other dolphins, but these cries aren't really the same thing as what we call talking. They can't discuss difficult problems with one another in the same way that people can. But dolphins do seem to have a sort of language that's made up of several different kinds of sounds. They can make sounds to call one another together, for instance, or to tell one another where food is.

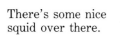 There's some nice squid over there.

Sometimes we can hear their cries when they're above the surface. When they're underwater we can't.

Peep!

Hey, Mommy, wait for me!

Kiyomi

❓ What Are These Things Doing?

Look! This is a fish, but it can live outside the water.

◄ This mudskipper has climbed up onto a tree. It climbs onto rocks or branches when the tide comes in. It uses its fins to get around.

◄ This filefish is looking for something to eat. The filefish blows the sand and stirs it up as it looks for things hiding there.

▲ A puddingwife hides itself in the sand.

◄ A puddingwife is sleeping. Before it goes to sleep the puddingwife covers itself with sand like a blanket. Fish have no eyelids, so their eyes stay open when they're asleep.

Here we see a striped prawn helping a fish to get clean. The fish doesn't move until the cleaning job is finished.

I thought it was eating the fish!

This round mask crab is holding up a shell to hide itself so that its enemies won't see it. Everywhere these crabs go they carry a shell around with them. They use it like a mask or a disguise, or to hide behind.

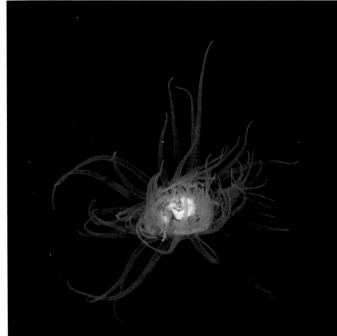

The pink sea anemone usually fastens itself to something hard like a rock. But when it wants to move it lets go and swims away. The photo at the lower left is very unusual, because it shows a sea anemone swimming along the same way a jellyfish does.

◀▲ Above, the anemone is attached. On the left it is swimming away.

● **To the Parent**

The mudskipper is an amphibious fish that lives on tidal flatlands. It can move about on land, where it breathes air carried in its gill chambers. Most sea anemones do not swim, remaining anchored by a pedal disc to a solid object. They can move slowly by enlarging the disc, but the swimming sea anemone and pink sea anemone can swim.

Whose Beak Is This?

■ The sea eagle's

The eagle's beak has a sharp hook at the end to tear apart the flesh of the animals it eats.

■ The Caribbean flamingo's

Flamingos put their beaks into the water and filter out tiny plants and animals to eat.

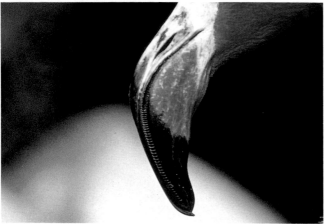

■ The toucan's

The toucan's colorful beak is large and looks very heavy. But actually the beak is spongy inside, making it very lightweight.

• **To the Parent**

The sharply curved beak of carnivorous birds like the eagle is very useful in tearing the flesh of their prey. The flamingo's beak has a sievelike structure inside enabling the bird to filter plankton out of the water. A toucan's beak is made up of a porous substance with many pockets of air, so it is not as heavy as it might appear.

Growing-Up Album

Who's Talking?

All the animals on these pages are talking, but which one is saying what? Look at the words they've said, then find the animals that said them. Trace a line with your finger to connect each animal with what it said.

Hare

Frog

Orangutan

Electric eel

Butterfly

1 My coat turns white in the winter.

2 I catch insects with my tongue.

3 I use electricity to catch fish.

4 My long arms help me to get around.

5 Those aren't my real eyes!

6 I can stuff a lot of acorns into my mouth.

7 I have shellfish for my dinner.

Spider

Dolphin

Prairie dog

Sea otter

Chipmunk

8 I'll eat any kind of grass at all.

9 I spin my web and wait for insects.

10 I eat fish in the ocean.

1 Hare, 2 Frog, 3 Electric eel, 4 Orangutan, 5 Butterfly,
6 Chipmunk, 7 Sea otter, 8 Prairie dog, 9 Spider, 10 Dolphin

Which Are the Real Shadows?

On these two pages you see pictures of four animals. There are a lot of shadows here, too. Look carefully and find the shadows that belong to those four animals.

① ② ③ ④ ⑤ ⑥

Sparrow: 15, Bat: 8, Crane: 13, Fox: 7

Where Do They Stay?

Which ones live in the ocean and which ones live in fresh water? See where they're hiding.

Ocean

Crawfish

Starfish

Catfish

Pond

Frog

Sea urchin

Octopus

Animals that live in the water usually
stay in a particular place. The ones
that live in the ocean don't go
into fresh water, and vice versa.
Ocean: sea urchin, octopus, starfish.
Pond: crawfish, frog, catfish.

A Child's First Library of Learning

Animals in Action

TIME
LIFE ®

Time-Life Books is a division of
Time Life Inc., a wholly owned
subsidiary of The Time Inc. Book Company
Time-Life Books, Alexandria, Virginia
Children's Publishing

Director: Robert H. Smith
Associate Director: R. S. Wotkyns III
Editorial Director: Neil Kagan
Promotion Director: Kathleen Tresnak
Editorial Consultants: Jacqueline A. Ball
                                 Andrew Gutelle

Editorial Supervision by:
International Editorial Services Inc.
Tokyo, Japan

Editor: C. E. Berry
Editorial Research: Miki Ishii
Design: Kim Bolitho
Writer: Pauline Bush
Educational Consultants: Janette Bryden
                                 Laurie Hanawa
Translation: Ronald K. Jones

Library of Congress Cataloging in Publication Data
Animals in action.
     p.   cm. — (A Child's first library of learning)
   Summary: Questions and answers, photographs, drawings,
cartoon characterizations, charts, and diagrams provide
information on physical properties and behavior of animals.
   ISBN 0-8094-4869-6.   ISBN 0-8094-4870-X (lib. bdg.)
   1. Animals—Miscellanea—Juvenile literature.
[1. Animals—Miscellanea.   2. Questions and answers.]
I. Time-Life Books.   II. Series.
QL49.A588 1989   591.5—dc19   88-36634
©1988 Time-Life Books Inc.
©1983 Gakken Co. Ltd.

Fourth printing 1992. Printed in U.S.A.
Published simultaneously in Canada.

TIME-LIFE is a trademark of Time Warner Inc. U.S.A.

Cover: Bob and Clara Calhoun/Bruce Coleman, Inc., New York